BILLY'S NARROW ESCAPE

By

Roger Shinnick

FOREWORD

This book is based on a true story and exemplifies Walkin N Circles Ranch's mission. WNCR exists to rescue, rehabilitate and provide proper care and humane treatment to unwanted, abused and abandoned horses. Their purpose is to provide each rescued horse humane and caring attention in which fear and pain are left at the front gate. Following a total assessment, gentle rehabilitation, training, and a rigorous screening process, WNCR endeavors to find loving adoptive homes for each horse. The objective is to provide each rescued horse a chance for a new start in a useful and productive life.

Dedication

Billy's story is not unique. Every year there are approximately 170,000 unwanted, abandoned, abused and starved horses in the United States. This book is dedicated to them, as well as to the families and children who want to help, and to the rescue organizations across the country like WNCR that are saving horses every day.

Charles R. Graham
Executive Director

New Mexico Horse Rescue at Walkin N Circles Ranch, Inc.®

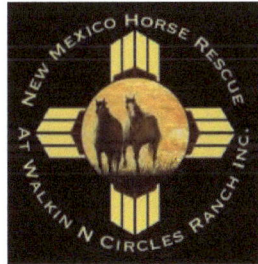

Contents

CHAPTER 1 – FREEDOM

The sun's rays reflected on the blanket of pure white snow that still covered the southern Colorado prairie. It had been a wet winter. Snow crystals dazzled the eye in the sunlight like tree ornaments. It was a peaceful time for all.

The slightly-higher temperature began the slow process of melting the frozen rivers and creeks that coursed through the valley. The snowmelt created trickles of water that striped the icy slopes and created pools of fresh water for the wildlife.

One of the larger beasts, the elk, roamed the country side. These strong and imposing animals clustered together with the bull overseeing his harem, in the hope that new life would arrive in the spring to preserve the herd. Their tan hide stood out in contrast to the white background and would alert hunters if they were around. So, they were cautious and used the trees and other vegetation as camouflage.

Photo courtesy of Rocky Mountain National Park

Despite the cold temperatures, blue jays flitted from tree to tree in their hunt for acorns, berries and seeds. The jays cawed with excitement as they competed with the squirrels and chipmunks for the prized morsels to carry them through the remaining days of winter. Foxes and their kits scampered in the snow in search of mice and ground squirrels before retreating to their dens. The bears had not left their winter dens.

Farms dotted the landscape against the white backdrop. The weathered houses and barns stood like guards against the chill winds that blew through the area.

The snow-packed roads were mostly silent. The farmers and ranchers were occupied indoors working on and repairing their equipment and tools in preparation for the spring plantings and grounds maintenance. They fed, watered and checked on their livestock throughout the day. If time permitted, they would saddle their horses and ride them through the valley, where many spots provided spectacular views of the distant frosted mountains. Trails were still visible as the deer used the same paths to reach the green foliage which had begun to peek through the snow.

The scenery was so tranquil and beautiful. No one would suspect that anything could disturb such peacefulness.

A band of wild horses gathered around the protective trees in the nearby forests. The San Juan Mountain range had received an exceptionally heavy snowfall during the night. The spruce, pine and ponderosa trees with their broad branches sheltered many animals that sought protection from the winds.

The mustangs had travelled many miles in hopes of finding grasses, broadleaf plants, and soil minerals they needed to sustain themselves. The sky was clearing, and offered the warming sun, exposing the vegetation they sought. The overhead snow-laden branches dropped moisture that collected into pools of fresh water. The horses lapped it up contentedly as they knew that today was a good day for them. The surrounding area was abundant in food and water, which they fed on during this break in the weather.

The mustangs saw a herd of mule deer nearby, also feeding on the emerging greenery. The deer's broad ears and short tails twitched with contentment as they grazed. The valley was a good place to eat, offering more than the northern area where they had been.

Photo Courtesy of Rocky Mountain National Park

The mustangs in the band numbered about twenty. A stallion took up his post on one side of the perimeter of the band to keep wolves and mountain lions away, a challenging task. He moved often to keep watch all around the band for intruders. The horse's keen sense of smell and hearing would alert him if any predator drew too near. He listened intently for any sounds which might signal a threat to the band. While his large eyes could see almost 350 degrees, he would adjust his head to focus on objects ahead as well.

Wolves posed a serious threat to the horses. A pack of wolves could easily wear down the larger animal in a chase, especially if it was old or very young. While the wolf could survive on berries and other plants, they would feverishly pursue a horse great distances as they were carnivores (meat eaters).

However, an even more threatening predator was the mountain lion. Their speed and agility surpassed any threat the wolf could present. The lion did not need to run in packs to gain an advantage. Once a horse had been singled out, he could not outrun a lion's speed nor escape his lethal claws and teeth. Instead, the horse band avoided these predators by not going into the high country where the cats hunted for their prey. No mountain lion had been sighted since the band had moved to the prairie, so luck was on their side for this migration. But, in the wild, the animals must remain ever watchful.

But a lone wolf had been stalking the band ever since they had left Wyoming. He had been successful in snatching three newborn foals so far. Since it was over a week since his last kill, the wolf must strike again soon. He would be hungry and determined to kill again. However, the stallion and the other mustangs were alert for the wolf's return.

Two mares, who had given birth to foals the previous night, stayed under the protective cover of the nearby trees. Mares and foals now rested in the safety of their crude shelter, where the mares' bodies surrounded the newborns to provide warmth. The foals suckled frequently to gain as much nourishment and strength as possible. The first forty-eight hours would be critical to determine if the foals would withstand the rest of the winter cold.

In the southernmost part of the band, the lead stallion detected the wolf scent and snorted loudly to the other horses. The lead mare looked up and faced the stallion with puzzlement. She had been moving the other horses to the best places to feed. Her initial confusion changed to fear as she stood erect, waiting for the stallion's command. The stallion was surprised to know that the predator was boldly looking for its prey during the day. Apparently, his hunger was driving him to take greater risks than usual. Night-time attacks were far more common, when the wolf could more easily surprise his prey. The muscular stallion moved his thousand pound body to face the predator, flattened his ears, flared his nostrils and stomped his front hooves. It was the same lone wolf. The stallion was determined not to lose another foal, although he knew that the wolf, though smaller, was very cunning and could move more swiftly.

Suddenly, the grey and black striped wolf made its move. He approached the band from upwind, going unseen thus far. His empty stomach urged him to face danger regardless of the consequences. He ran from tree to tree to avoid being seen. The wolf's heart pounded and his breathing accelerated as he drew nearer to the sheltering trees. He zeroed in on the weakest foal, which was looking at his mother. The day-old colt had trouble nursing and was hungry. He did not understand why his mother had shaken suddenly causing the foal to lose hold of the mare's teat.

Photo Courtesy of Gary Kramer US Fish and Wildlife Service

Although the other horses were alerted by the stallion's alarm, the mares chose not to flee, since the newborns were still too weak to run. The mares rose quickly to their feet, prepared to defend their foals. They pushed the newborns to the back of the protective thicket of trees and bravely stood their ground. However, this defensive action did not deter the wolf.

The star-faced mare was the first to see the intruder. The wolf's cold, steel look and menacing eyes sent chills through her body. She whinnied a loud warning and reared, lashing out wildly with her hooves. In only a few seconds the large-fanged wolf was able to grab her screaming, helpless foal. The mare struck out to kill the wolf but her frantic, flailing hooves did not make contact. The wolf clamped his jaws around the hind legs of the foal and dragged him ten feet. The wolf was about to grab the foal by the neck and break its spine, when the mare's crazed snorting and kicking caused the wolf to glance up – a fatal mistake. The wolf took its attention away from the foal for only a few seconds, but it was enough for another mare to intercede. She was a taller, heavier, amber-colored horse whose coat was drenched with sweat. She would foal soon and knew if she didn't stop this attack, her foal would eventually become the wolf's next target. She reared up on her hind legs despite her heavy girth and kicked the wolf a glancing blow, enough to stun him and loosen his grip on the screaming foal.

Suddenly, the stallion crashed through the nearby trees, sending large broken branches in every direction. He struck the wolf at a gallop with fury in his eyes. The impact launched the wolf into the air and onto a pile of broken timber. The wolf made a feeble attempt to get up and evade his pursuer, but the stallion was relentless in cornering the wolf and delivered several quick and fatal kicks. The wolf did not move. He would not kill again.

The star-faced mare quickly reached the injured foal and licked it tenderly. Fortunately, the cuts to its hind legs were not deep. The foal nickered in delight as the mare continued to clean its wounds. He finally struggled to his feet and the mare knew that she succeeded in saving her baby with the help of the stallion. The foal was wobbly and in some pain as he stood but suckled contentedly. The rich, nourishing milk fed and comforted him. The foal knew that for this moment he was safe and protected.

The amber-colored mare was joined by two other pregnant mares, who stood by and witnessed the bonding between the star-faced mare and her bruised foal. Such nurturing reminded them that they would soon have foals of their own. The tree sanctuary offered a good place for them to foal as well. They had no idea that their fates were about to change.

Photo Courtesy of Theodore National Park

The stallion continued to stand over the dead wolf, whinnying loudly. He was proud of what he had done. He then moved into the nearby hills a short distance away and faced the mares. He stood boldly, letting his stance tell them that he was their leader and protector.

Despite his strength and confidence the stallion could not be aware that he had yet to meet his worst danger. He would soon learn about an even more deadly threat, one who walked on two legs called "man."

CHAPTER 2 – BLM

Picture Courtesy of BLM.gov

Three hundred miles away in Denver, Colorado, the Bureau of Land Management (BLM) was hosting a public meeting to discuss how to address the large number of wild horses on public lands. George Willard, the Western Regional Director, opened the meeting and stated. "Ladies and gentlemen, The BLM has gathered data about the numbers of wild horses roaming in Wyoming, Nevada, Colorado, and New Mexico and we have determined that we must initiate another series of horse round ups. The first will occur in the Southern Colorado and Northern New Mexico flat lands. The lack of moisture there for the last three years is the principle cause for our need to take this action."

Before George could continue, several people in the audience raised their hands. "I see we have questions."

"Mr. Willard." The first man said. "Isn't it more natural to leave these animals in the wild?"

George said. "Well, yes, ideally. However, we need to ask ourselves, "Is it more humane to leave these magnificent animals to perish in the wild? The rate of fatality has been unusually high due to the drought. Unless we see a significant increase in moisture, the Bureau's position is to supplement their needs with water and hay. But when their numbers grow too large, then our policy is to relocate them and/or put them up for adoption."

A lady in the third row spoke next. She asked, "What is the fatality rate for horses in these roundups? Is there any way to changes the methods, so they cause less stress for the mustangs?"

George replied, "Actually, on the average, we lose very few animals. Of course, even a few is regrettable and we are striving to reduce even that number. In our roundups, we use helicopters to carefully move the horses into collection pens. This is a more effective method in minimizing the run time for the animals, which lowers the chance for injuries. Once the horses are enclosed in these pens, we sort them by gender and age. Older horses go to long-term BLM ranches, and younger ones go back out to the open range or get put up for adoption."

A newspaper reporter from the local area raised her hand and asked, "What about the mares and foals who run in the stampede? Don't they get separated?"

George stated. "Yes. On occasion they do. One of the jobs of the helicopter pilot is to watch out for this possibility. They radio the wranglers on the ground, who then work to reunite them."

The meeting continued for another hour. The proceedings ended with most attendees stating that they were still uneasy about the BLM policy for roundups. The Agency was facing budget cuts which made supplying feed for the wild herds less feasible. Leaving the starving animals on the open range without some intervention appeared to be an even less humane solution.

CHAPTER 3 – THE ROUND UP

Photo Courtesy of National Park Service

The weather had become unseasonably mild, so the horses remained in the valley near the San Juan Mountains. While night time temperatures continued to be cold, the sunny days warmed the land pleasantly. Three more mares birthed their foals, and the band watched as the new colts and fillies struggled to find their legs and wobble towards their mothers to nurse. The older horses showed some impatience when the energetic babies' soon began to kick and nip at each other and romp in the wildflowers. The seniors whinnied at the mothers to mind their youngsters.

Photo Courtesy of US Parks

Two months later, the band had migrated east to the open prairies in Southern Colorado, where they feasted on the fresh grasses that bloomed under the warm sun. Late winter rains had provided enough moisture for the grasslands to take on the look of an endless green carpet. The vegetation tasted sweet and the horses enjoyed the lush growth. While the stallion still patrolled the perimeter of the band, most horses felt secure enough to graze a little further afield. The mustangs had no idea that loud and threatening man-made machines would arrive soon and change their lives forever.

The distant dull humming sound grew ever louder as two helicopters broke through the clouds at midafternoon. They flew in formation to appear as large as possible. Their mission was to round up the thousand wild horses estimated by the BLM to be in the southern Colorado plains. These machines were fairly light, weighing only three thousand pounds, so their speed and maneuverability made them ideal for this task. The large rotating blades made a very loud whooshing noise, which could be heard for miles, echoing off nearby canyon walls. These aircraft could fly up to one hundred and fifty miles per hour and hover only 100 feet above the ground.

The two-seater helicopters with oval, clear windows looked like large grasshoppers with bulbous heads as they popped over the nearby hills. The sun's reflection off the hardened glass accentuated their threatening look. The mustangs anxiously searched the sky for the source of the roar.

At first the mustangs froze in place. But then the stallion reared and urged the band to flee. The band's movement became disorganized, as the horses searched for a common escape route. Dirt and small rocks flew and the ground shook from the panicked animals. Mares gathered their foals in close, as the band moved quickly. The horses looked for the stallion, who was running south. Once the horses spotted their leader, they changed their direction and followed him. They looked to him for their safety. The stallion had earned the band's confidence in the past by warding off nature's dangers in the wild.

Other bands of horses came into view as the aircraft drove the various groups of animals from long distances onto a common path. The lack of familiarity with the horses in other bands disturbed some of the animals, as the mares, foals and yearlings wanted to stay within their "family." However, the threatening sounds drove them to run as fast as they could and not stay within their individual bands. They would now become just a greater mass of animals.

The helicopters maintained their elevation at one hundred feet and slowed their speed. They were under strict orders from the federal government to avoid causing harm to the horses. The helicopters herded the horses toward the open canyon, where large corrals had been set up. Wranglers on horseback positioned themselves along the route to keep straying horses from doubling back to escape.

Their plan worked. The lead stallion of each band kept ahead of the other mustangs in his family, which ensured the horses followed efficiently down the canyon and made the job of the helicopters and wranglers easier. In addition to the mustangs, other breeds of horses were present. Owners of these animals had abandoned them to the wild, which contributed to the ever growing numbers of horses that the environment could no longer support.

With only a mile left to the collection pens, the contractor released a "Judas Horse." This highly trained mare ran alongside the lead stallion of the front band, who was tiring and thus allowed another horse to share the leadership position. Their strong and powerful strides radiated confidence. The bands didn't question the direction they were heading. Everyone trusted their judgment because they were clearly outrunning those horrible machines. They maintained the speed that would drive all the horses into the waiting corrals. There was so much dust from the horses' hooves that the stallion could not see the distant fences, which would trap his herd.

The run was not without injury. The amber colored mare witnessed a companion pregnant mare fall into a narrow arroyo. Ignoring the rest of the herd and the calls from the nearby wranglers, she remained with the mare who lay in the sand, unable to get up. Although she knew that there was nothing she could do to help, she stayed with her until she saw the wrangler approach. She whinnied a farewell, and then rejoined the galloping herd.

The Chase

As soon as the animals got boxed into the pens, the wrangler called for the "Judas Horse" to return to the side of the canyon. The lead stallion reacted to the "Judas Horse" leaving, as he thought this mare had joined his herd. He tried to follow her out of the pen but was waived off by the wranglers' lassos. The stallion charged the gate and splintered it with his kicks. Other horses in the pen reacted to the commotion and reared up. The wranglers witnessed the panic but quietly stood their ground.

The horses gradually began to settle down. Wranglers brought out hay and water, which helped calm them.

The star-faced mare looked around for her colt but did not see him. In the rush to get to the pens she had lost track of her foal. The speed was too much for the little horse to keep up, and he fell behind. Frantically, the mare whinnied and whinnied, calling to him. Her breathing became more and more labored with repeated blowing sounds and flaring nostrils. She was clearly agitated and desperately moved her head back and forth in hopes of detecting his unique scent.

The three pregnant mares that had stayed close to her during the run lifted their heads to look for the missing foal as well. They scanned their crowded pen but he was not there.

Suddenly, the mare heard a familiar cry from the next pen. His cry was unmistakable to his mother, who paced back and forth at the fence closest to the foal's pen. The foal approached his mother but did not understand why the fence separated them. He cried as he gazed at her. He wanted his mother and he wanted her now!

Fortunately, one of the wranglers was in the area as he checked on the horses. As he walked near the pen where the foal was crying, he recognized the little animal's desperate state. He went to him, put on a halter with a lead rope, and walked him around in hopes of finding his mother. When he got to the adjacent pen, the star-faced mare trotted over immediately and whinnied her plea. Her agitation and cries convinced him that this mare must be the foal's mother. He opened the gate and released him, then stood back and witnessed their happy reunion.

CHAPTER 4 – TRANSPORT

The wranglers kept the horses in the collection pens for a week. By then, the animals' strength was restored, which was needed for the next event, an onerous trip to a new location. Being provided hay and water was a welcome change from having to look for their food in the wild. The star-faced mare and her newborn foal along with the other three pregnant mares, stayed close together. The events of the past week had been frightening for them.

The days were getting warmer and the animals settled down to this new routine. The most troublesome things to deal with were the flies that became more numerous as the temperatures rose. Swishing tails and a shake of the head took care of many of the bothersome insects. Two horses were often seen standing head to tail beside each other, using their tails to swish the pesky flies from one another's face and eyes.

The next day the horses heard machinery noises again. At first they looked up to see if the whirling "monsters" had returned. But only a flock of big black birds could be seen against the milky white skies. The horses grew restless as the noise grew louder.

Dust rose in the distance. Huge semis rolled in, spewing rocks and dirt in their wake. They were attached to double level livestock trailers. The horses became alarmed. Their nostrils flared and the whites of their eyes showed as they anxiously pawed the ground.

Livestock Trailer - Photo Courtesy of Roger Shinnick

The wranglers set up narrow passageways and began to release the horses from the pens into the trailers. The horses looked for a way to be set free. But, the gate led to a chute discharging the horses into the huge, dark and forbidding trailer. The bottom level had more height than the upper deck. The horses assigned to the second level had to lower their heads, as there was not enough room for them to stand upright. They had to stay in that position for the length of the trip.

As the trailers filled, one could hear the fear in the snorts and screams of the horses. These trucks were extremely confining and the horses sensed their loss of freedom forever. The massive rigs would normally have different destinations, which included long term care locations for non-adoptable horses and short term locations for adoptable horses. But, not this herd – they were going to a sale barn for auction.

The star-faced mare and her colt were lucky. Even though their quarters were cramped on the first level, they were still together. However, when one horse shifted position, the other horses had to move as well. The mare snorted if another horse bumped or got too close to her little foal. The three pregnant mares were not nearby and she wondered if she would ever see them again.

The giant vehicles travelled at night to avoid unnecessary attention. The engines groaned as they hauled their heavy loads. Dark exhaust from the diesel-powered trucks spewed into the night air.

Many of the captured horses were not wild, but were from ranches and farms where they had lived for years until their owners no longer wanted them. The horses' eyes showed their fear and bewilderment. They had been given strong and respectful names. How does one abandon an animal they have named "King," or "Chief," or "Beauty," or "Dancer"? They were bays, appaloosas, buckskins, paints and palominos.

Photo Courtesy of Roger Shinnick

Not too long ago their owners had valued these fine creatures as race horses, trail horses, or show horses, whose blood lines produced valuable foals. Many had earned prize money for their owners, who decorated their ranch homes with blue ribbons and trophies. They were loved and respected. They had served their masters well.

But, something had changed. People suddenly altered their lives and no longer wanted them. The horses left their comfortable surroundings for the wild and now this. They wanted to strike out and escape but couldn't. They had no voice; they had no choice.

The horses were doomed. A trip to a sale barn meant that most would be sold for slaughter.

CHAPTER 5 – THE SALE BARN

The sale barn sat near the edge of a rural New Mexican town. Its huge size dominated the agricultural area. Inside, there were a hundred pens that held up to ten horses each. The building was dimly lit, a threatening sign for these poor animals.

The trucks arrived as the sun rose. A refreshing wind blew through the cramped and smelly trailers. The wranglers unloaded the trucks and moved the horses into the pens. The handlers separated the animals by size, breed and whether mares had foals or were pregnant.

Despite numerous pregnant mares in the herd, the sale barn manager did not separate them from the auction. He was familiar with the State animal cruelty laws and chose not to consider their sale as mistreatment. If he could get a few more sold, it was more money for him.

Suddenly, the star-face mare saw the three pregnant mares in the pen next to her and whinnied to get their attention. She was afraid of the dark surroundings and seeing them helped her calm down a little.

Rain was pelting the roof of the barn. Leaks from the roof created muddy areas in the pens. The horses were hungry and thirsty as they had not received food or water during the long trip.

Finally, water began to flow into the troughs in the pens. Horses crowded one another to get their first drink in almost ten hours. Wagons made their way down the main aisles of the barns, with handlers throwing out flakes of feed. The horses looked up hopefully and hungrily. Little did they know that this station was the last stop for most of them, before kill-buyers hauled them to a slaughterhouse in Mexico.

The auction commenced in the late afternoon. Bleachers were crowded with buyers, who traveled long distances to participate in an event that featured the largest roundup of wild horses so far that year. The company that had collected the herds from the southern Colorado prairie had done a good job; very few injuries had occurred. The sale barn manager paraded the horses in groups of ten. The bids were vigorous and vocal. "Kill-buyers," who represented the interests of investors to send horses to slaughterhouses in Mexico, outnumbered the ranchers. The roundup had brought so many horses for sale that the starting price per head was unusually low, which fed the excitement of the kill-buyers. They hoped for sizeable profits.

A rancher, who specialized in trail rides, bid and won the purchase of the star-faced mare and her foal. They and ten other horses would be on their way to Arizona. They were the lucky ones. They would be the only horses not marked for slaughter that day.

The three pregnant mares appeared in the next lot of ten horses. The bidding was about to begin, when a rancher objected to their inclusion in the auction. While he could not afford to buy them, he pleaded that their sale be delayed to allow horse rescues in New Mexico purchase them. The sale barn manager did not want to make a fuss, considering the several hundred horses to be auctioned off. The rancher was a regular customer at the sale barn and the manager did not want to offend him.

Wranglers moved the mares back to their pens. The sale barn manager was unhappy about this disruption. His commission was based on the volume of completed sales. The delay of the auction and the expense to keep the mares until the foals were born would have an impact on his earnings.

A total of fourteen pregnant mares were at risk. The circumstances were dire, since any foals separated from their mothers would die for lack of the mare's nourishing milk.

Horse rescue ranches throughout New Mexico showed interest in saving the mares but the sale barn stipulated that they would hold the mares only five days once the foals were born. So, a notice was sent out on the internet announcing the plight of the mares. Only kill-buyers were interested in bidding for these mares once they had their foals. They would abandon the foals and let them perish, as they would have no use for these poor creatures.

Four Corners Equine Rescue

Image courtesy of the Four Corner's Equine Rescue

Four Corners Equine Rescue sent out the following notice on the internet in March, 2011, making a plea for donations:

Help the Pregnant Mares

Fourteen mares are headed for Mexico if we do not raise the money to save them. Eleven of the mares are pregnant, and three have brand new foals…Once born, the foals will not survive the trip, if they are loaded onto the transport. We have until Friday, March 18, 2011, to raise the funds to purchase them and remove them from the property. They are currently at a sale barn…we must raise $3600 before Friday!! [1]

---

[1]*Help the Pregnant Mares,* (accessed May 26, 2014), available from http://www.fourcornersequinerescue.org/slaughtermaresrescue.html

The plea prompted enough donations for the lead rescue ranch to purchase thirty animals, of which, eleven were pregnant. According to New Mexico livestock law, pregnant mares cannot be sold for slaughter. Three mares had newborn foals. Walkin N Circles Ranch (WNCR) received notice that they would be receiving two pregnant mares and a mare with a newborn foal.

Photo Courtesy of the New Mexico Livestock Board

A New Mexico Livestock Board Inspector hitched the large horse trailer to the Super Duty truck and left for the sale barn. He was pleased that he would be able to save the animals.

The truck and hitched trailer reached the sale barn lots by midafternoon. Very few animals remained, as the transports to Mexico had removed the doomed horses much earlier. March snow flurries had left a sprinkling of white flakes that encrusted the parking lot. The crackling of frozen mud and small pools of ice announced the arrival of the NMLB truck and trailer.

A sale barn employee approached the NMLB inspector and inquired about his reason for being there.

"Hey, we are done with the auction, what is it now?"

The Inspector looked up and remarked. "For your information, I understand that you were trying to sell pregnant mares at last week's auction. You realize that such action is a violation of State law. Frank Lawson, another NMLB inspector, was here and he has already submitted a report to the State office for action. You can expect to go with your boss to Santa Fe soon and explain yourself. In the meantime, I am taking the remaining mares and any newborn foals."

The scruffy employee realized that he should not have tried to challenge the Inspector. His boss already told him that repeated violations of the livestock law could shut down their operation and he would be out of a job.

The mares looked up nervously from their dark stalls and wondered if the Inspector would harm them. The past two weeks had been filled with one traumatic event after another, when other men had caused them great fear.

The Inspector approached the mares slowly with halters and lead ropes slung over his arm. He realized that safely moving them to the trailer would take some time. He stood still and looked at the horses respectfully. He talked softly to them and slowly moved closer, as the mares began to show less agitation. Half an hour later, he had haltered the horses, and then quietly walked them around the deserted parking lot before approaching the trailer. Surprisingly, the actual loading of the horses into the trailer went smoothly. The mare with the newborn foal entered first, followed by the two pregnant mares.

CHAPTER 6 – THE RESCUED MARES ARRIVE AT WALKIN' N CIRCLES RANCH

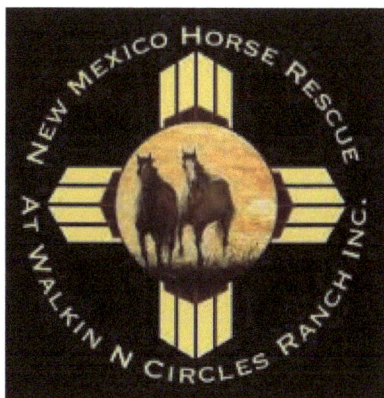
Image Courtesy of WNCR

The weather improved dramatically as the truck and trailer headed northward. The Inspector could hear the horses whinny in the trailer but the sounds were soft. The feed bin for each stall was full of fresh hay for the three hour ride. The animals settled down comfortably.

The transport reached WNCR by late afternoon. The weather was noticeably warmer with only a slight breeze. The sunny surroundings were pleasant and inviting.

Several ranch hands gathered to welcome the mares and the little foal. The horses backed out of the trailers safely and inspected the immediate area outside the trailer. Other horses nearby neighed their welcome.

Photo Courtesy of WNCR

Ranch hands named the three mares: Amber, Sunny Girl and Biscuit. Amber, the dark brown mare, was in labor when she arrived at the Ranch. Sunny Girl, a light brown mare, was with her foal but it was clear that her baby was very weak. It had trouble standing up and only managed to do so when needing to nurse. Biscuit, a sorrel or brownish orange mare, was the most calm of the three. An examination showed that she wasn't due for another two weeks.

The ranch hands led Amber into a stall, with fresh straw bedding laid in anticipation of the birth. While she was less agitated, her big black eyes still showed suspicion. Her labor alone would account for nervousness, but she could not forget what she had gone through in the last two weeks. She had fond memories of the forest and prairies, where she was free to feed on lush green growth. Despite the harshness of the weather in the wild, she missed the freedom which was no longer hers. The ranch hands here were kind to her, but they looked just like the people who had managed the roundup, the transport and the auction barn. It was "man" who operated those big and noisy machines that drove her friends into ditches, never to return. It was "man" who drove the big rigs that hauled the crying horses to slaughter in Mexico. Her instinct told her to flee as soon as she could. She was not ready to give up her wildness. The mare eyed the ranch hands suspiciously until they had left her stall.

The ranch foreman checked on the mare at midnight but the mare had not yet delivered. The mare kept a quiet vigil while she waited for the birth.

The foal arrived during the night. His light tan coat showed in sharp contrast to his mother's dark brown hide.

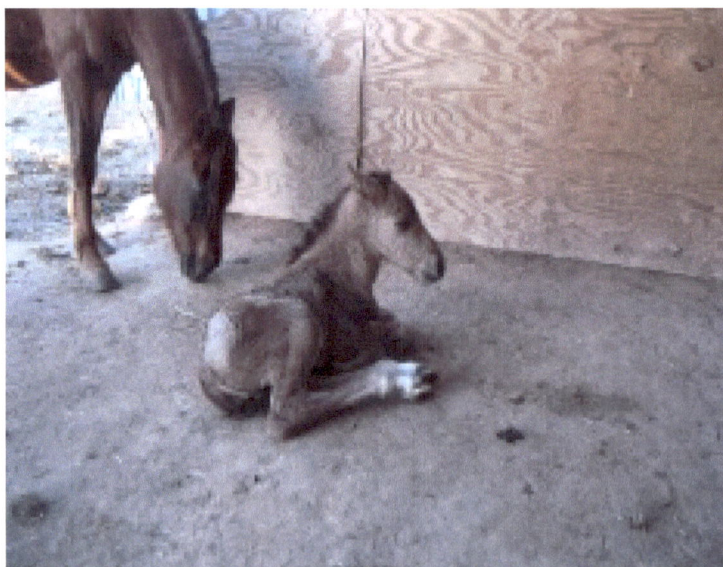
Photo Courtesy of WNCR

Any concerns about Amber not being a good mom quickly vanished. She devoted tireless attention to her newborn, who bonded with her immediately.

The foal was named "Billy," because long whiskers appeared on his chin from the first day. It reminded the ranch hands of a Billy Goat. His pretty light coat and Amber's darker brown color presented a beautiful contrast.

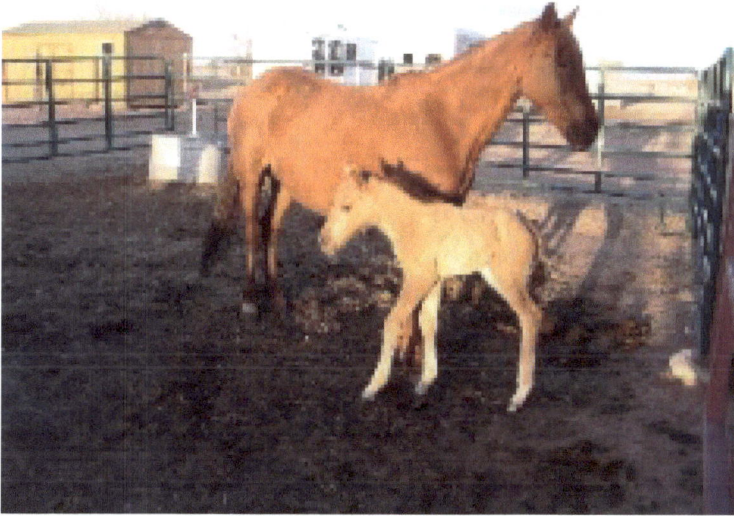

Photo Courtesy of WNCR

Amber was a very protective mom, who closely watched any ranch hand who entered her corral. In turn, the ranch hands respected Amber's space. They knew she had suffered traumatic experiences before she arrived at Walkin N Circles Ranch. And, as a mustang, she was unaccustomed to being restricted. It would take some time before her wildness would leave her, if it ever would.

CHAPTER 7 – SEPARATION

Billy stood next to Amber in the stall enjoying the bright sun and the warmth that radiated from the barn walls. He knew nothing of the fears his mother had suffered before he came into this world: the wolf attack in the wild, the alarming helicopters in the horse roundup, the wretched and confining transport for eight hours, the cold and dark holding pens at the sale barn, and the pains of labor before she could foal. Up to now his world was simple. He looked at her soft eyes and found only love. He wanted to be with her forever.

Amber and Billy stayed together in their corral for six months. Then it was time to wean the foal from his mother. Amber had been a good mom, teaching Billy the essential lessons in being a horse: how to eat hay, not to nibble on fence posts, and showing him how to communicate with other horses.

The day the ranch hand led Amber out of the corral Billy immediately protested with his loud cries. He did not understand why his mother was no longer with him. He cried for days after their separation.

"Baaaaaaaaaaaaaaaaaaaaaaaaaaaaah!"

After the third day, Billy was waiting for an opportunity to find his mother. A ranch hand had just come from Amber's corral, where she had groomed her. She came to fill Billy's water tank. Billy approached the ranch hand and smelled her gloves. He recognized his mother's odor! She must be nearby! He began to pace his stall anxiously. The ranch hand left Billy's area thinking all was well. But, the look in his eyes told a different story. The odor was too much for him. He had to find his mother!

Despite the fresh water and hay that would have kept him there, he decided it was time to find his mother. Billy leapt over the four foot gate to freedom and his mother.

"Wow. That was easy!" he thought. He ran past the other stalls. Once he was outside of the barn, he found Amber in another corral. She looked up at him with surprise, but quickly moved beside him at the fence. They nuzzled each other tenderly, nickering their love. An unexpected loose gate allowed Billy to enter the corral where Amber was. This was great…back with mom!

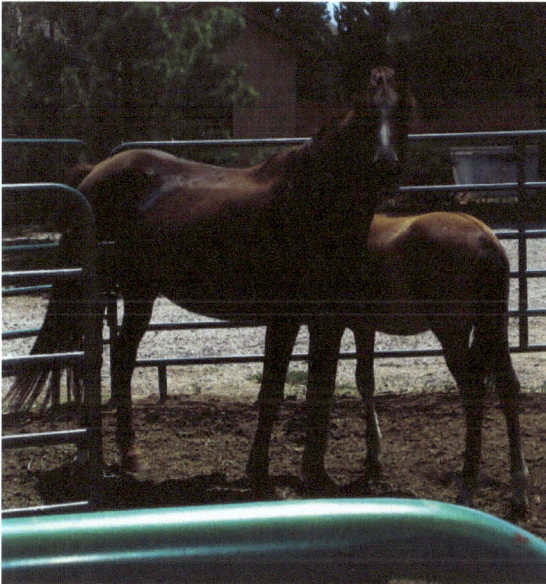

Photo Courtesy of WNCR

The ranch hands watched them for a long time. There was no rush to put Billy back in his stall. They knew that Billy missed his mom. On the other hand, it was important for horses to learn to be independent, or they would not survive. After a short visit, Billy was returned to his stall in the barn.

However, his first success prompted him to make a second escape, again by leaping over the gate. Jumping a four foot gate was almost unheard of for a foal, and told how athletic he was. It was a few days later that he tried this again. However, this time he did not find Amber, because she was no longer at the ranch. She had left for her new home the previous day. The corral she had been in was empty. His search of other nearby corrals also ended up with no mother. Finally, he stood there in silence. When the ranch hand came up and haltered him, he lowered his head and did not fight back.

After this, Billy was downcast for a time. Ranch hands spent more time with him and he loved to be groomed. He was taken on short walks around the ranch for exercise and received neighs and whinnies from many of the horses. It was if they were saying "It's okay to be here without your mom. We all went through the same thing." He began to form attachments to his new

corral mates.

CHAPTER 8 – BILLY MAKES A GOOD FRIEND WITH JEWEL.

Jewel
Photo Courtesy of WNCR

Jewel was born two weeks after Billy. Her mother, Biscuit, was one of the other pregnant mares rescued from the sale barn. Like Billy, Jewel developed into a healthy and sound horse with the care she received at Walkin N Circles. At birth, each of these foals weighed about a hundred pounds. Now that they were both approximately six months old, their weight had increased to over five hundred pounds each.

Billy and Jewel shared the same corral once the ranch hands had separated them from their mothers. Jewel also had a difficult time but sharing a corral with Billy helped her as well. Being young horses, they loved to frolic. Their best times were when the ranch hands took them to the arena where they could run joyfully and buck without a care. They felt as free as the birds that circled the ranch. The strong afternoon winds only made them more excited.

Jewel and Billy did have some differences just as all roommates did. Billy was known for taking a nap every morning about ten o'clock. He relished the warm sun that made him comfortable on the dusty ground. He would sleep so soundly that he was unaware of other horse activity in the corral. On one occasion Jewel decided to play a trick on Billy while he was asleep. She stirred up the other young horses, Houdini and Wyoming, who responded to Jewel's game. The three horses began to prance and act silly around Billy, who remained asleep in the middle of the corral. Finally, Billy woke up and snorted with irritation. He did not appreciate having his nap interrupted! The other horses were surprised, as they were just playing. Jewel walked off as if nothing had happened!

CHAPTER 9 – THE CIRCLE PEN

The horses liked leaving their corrals and taking walks around the ranch. One of the areas where they were taken for exercise was the circle pen, a thirty foot wide fenced-in work out area with a thick base of sand. The structure offered safe surroundings for the trainer to lunge a horse, i.e. run the horse at the end of a lead rope in a circular manner for training and exercise.

As young foals, the horses enjoyed a great amount of attention from ranch hands as well as visitors. Unfortunately, this also worked against them as they had not mentally developed as horses. Training was needed to manage their naturally high spirits. High energy and a weight of five hundred pounds for each young horse could spell problems for the humans handling them, if they did not receive proper training.

Billy met his trainer in late summer. He had been weaned for just over a week when the trainer selected him to enter the next phase of his life at WNCR, ground training. This was a mandatory first step before he could ever be considered for riding. Billy proved to be a good student. He learned quickly to be haltered, to walk beside a ranch hand, to stop, back up, move his hind quarters, and to flex his neck. Billy practiced these commands over and over with his trainer. His lessons were only about 20 minutes long. Just like a human baby, he could only pay attention for short periods of time.

Training was not all work. The trainer rewarded Billy for his hard work by scratching his withers, a raised area on his back just behind his mane. He loved it when the trainer scratched him there because he could not reach it himself.

Of course, Billy was not always the most attentive student. Like most inexperienced colts, he loved to look around to see what was going on. One particular time he watched the ranch foreman nearby using a tractor to move part of "poop mountain," a large mound of horse droppings. The foreman was shaping the area for the mushroom farmer who was coming soon to remove it. No matter how hard the trainer prompted him to lunge in the circle pen, Billy remained focused on the tractor. The maneuvering of the loud, red tractor with belching smoke held his attention much better than a mere trainer could! The trainer paused for a few minutes and waited for the foreman to finish his work. Then Billy became the good student again.

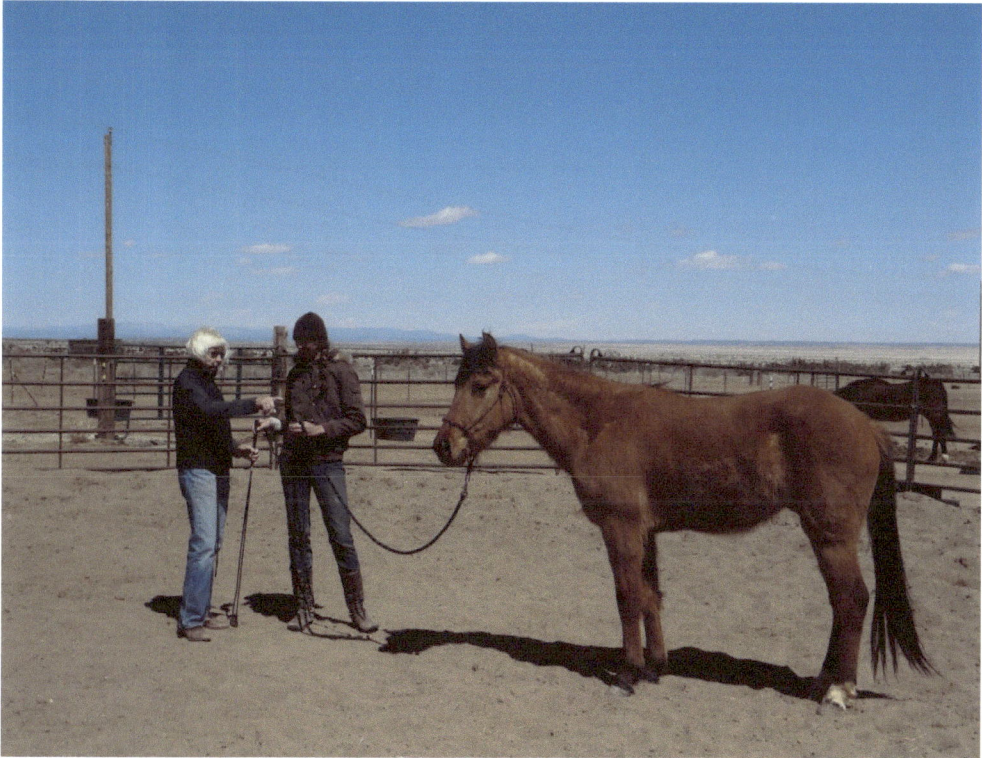

Jane and Kirsten training Billy
Photo Courtesy of WNCR

By the time Billy was two years old he had mastered ground training and was ready to be ridden. The trainer began the process by introducing a riding blanket. She carried the blanket over to Billy for him to smell at first. Since he did not react negatively, she proceeded to wave the blanket in front of him. He stood there and watched her carefully, always on the lookout for change. However, he accepted the blanket, which she then rubbed against his neck, shoulders and side. So far, so good. When the trainer placed it on his back, he jerked abruptly but then settled down. Additional lessons included the same routine until he could accept the blanket without even a twinge. The trainer then led him around the ranch with the blanket on his back like a distinguished gentleman wearing a fancy waistcoat.

Weeks later the trainer brought out a western saddle. Billy's confidence soon left him. The fifty pound beefy leather "thing" made Billy uncomfortable. He immediately moved and strained against the lead rope. The trainer removed the saddle and waited. Like the blanket, she moved very slowly with the introduction of the saddle. With encouragement and some soft rubs on his withers and neck, Billy allowed the trainer to put the saddle on him again. He finally accepted it, even after she fastened the cinch, a wide belt below Billy's belly. Additional lessons followed with the blanket and saddle on him. He performed all ground training drills without a problem with the additional weight. Billy got used to the new set of equipment and was ready for the next step, riding.

Photo Courtesy of Roger Shinnick

To curb Billy's fears, the trainer first just leaned against the saddle and then later, pressed down on the saddle to put additional weight on his back. Next, she climbed the circle pen fence, leaned over and pressed harder on the saddle from above. When Billy tolerated this change, she placed her leg on his saddle, while still holding on to the fence. The trainer repeated this drill for several lessons until Billy showed no reaction to this routine. Finally, after weeks of exposure to the blanket, saddle and pressure on the saddle at odd angles, Billy was ready for the next step.

The completion of the ground training and exposure to the blanket and saddle allowed the trainer to mount Billy without incident. The trainer began to ride Billy frequently. While the early riding events were limited to the circle pen, the trainer eventually took him into the arena a larger and less confined area. Several months later after intensive practice, Billy left the ranch's boundaries. He did well despite an occasional rolling sage brush or even the sight of a coyote. This predator was too small to worry about and only startled Billy a little. Billy stayed keenly attuned to his surroundings by moving his ears independently, turning them to the right or left like individual antennae picking up radio signals.

Photo Courtesy of National Park Service

CHAPTER 10 – BILLY MEETS CHAD

Billy loved being with people. When the Ranch gave tours to visitors, he always stood near the fence to be petted and pampered. He was proud of his beautiful light brown coat and dark mane and tail.

Billy loved to see the children visit the Ranch. The kindness in their eyes reminded him of the tenderness he had experienced with his mother. He still had fond memories of her, knowing that he would never see her again.

In September, a busload of children from a mid-school in Albuquerque visited WNCR. The field trip was the inspiration of a parent whose son was having difficulty in school. Chad's lack of interest in studying and socializing began when he had received the news that his father, a Marine, had died in Afghanistan.

His mother came up with the field trip idea after she saw a Walkin N Circles Horse Rescue poster on one of Chad's bedroom walls. A year before, the family had visited Weem's Artfest at the New Mexico Fairgrounds. Walkin N Circles Horse Rescue Ranch had a booth there and Chad had talked to a ranch volunteer while his parents toured the art exhibits. When they returned, he had the Ranch poster as well as some brochures. He was very excited and pleaded with his parents to visit the ranch, but time had run out and his father had been deployed.

Photo Courtesy of Roger Shinnick

Every time Chad saw the ranch billboard on Interstate 40, he reminded his mother of her promise to visit the ranch. In looking back, his mother wished that she had brought Chad to the ranch before. Maybe that would have helped him overcome the grief he now felt because of the loss of his dad.

A slight breeze was blowing from the west as the packed school bus rolled to a stop in the WNCR parking lot. When the kids got off the bus, they gazed around in wonder at the splendor of the Sandia Mountains in the distance and the flat prairie in front of them. Many of the children had not had the opportunity to leave the city or experience the outdoors away from the hustle and bustle of the metropolitan area.

Several ranch hands greeted the children and explained the mission of the ranch: to rescue abused and abandoned horses. Without hesitation, the group went over to see some of the "horse ambassadors," Storm and Heat. Their soft expressions said "come on over, we like people!"

Storm and Heat
Photo Courtesy of WNCR

The kids were amazed by the number of teams that worked to make operating the ranch a success. Volunteers helped with paperwork, feeding, health issues, education, training, and ranch grounds. There was lots of work to be done! They learned that keeping water tanks clean, full and free of ice was one of the highest priorities during the winter. Each horse drank six to eight gallons per day.

Nearby a group of volunteers was unloading a hay truck. Each bale weighed about seventy pounds and getting the bales as close together as possible was important to keep the hay fresh. Moldy hay would make horses very sick. The morning sun felt good as the ranch hands worked together to complete this important job. The ranch brought in large truckloads of hay several times a year to feed the hundred horses. The timing was important to take advantage of the cost and availability. So, when the truck arrived many hands were needed to stack and protect the hay.

Photo Courtesy of WNCR

Chad was quiet during the tour. The forty students followed the two ranch hands, who held their interest with many, interesting real life stories about the ranch.

One of the hands named Ed asked, "Does anyone know how horses digest hay?" The group of kids grew quiet as they looked among themselves for someone to answer the question. No one raised their hands for a few minutes.

Finally, Chad, who had been reading up on horse behavior and nutrition said. "Horses eat plants like hay, alfalfa and other grasses because their digestive system is made specially to handle such things. Cows have four stomachs to help them digest their food. Horses have only one, but it's off to the side. They also have an appendix like ours but it's much bigger. It helps the horse digest its food."

"Chad. Thank you very much. You obviously know something about horses."

The ranch hand asked further. "Can anyone tell me how long a horse spends grazing or looking for food per day?"

A quick hand rose up. It was Lucille, whose grandpa had horses in Tijeras, a nearby town. She said. "I think its eight hours per day."

The ranch hand said. "You're very close. They do spend several hours per day looking for food but we typically limit their time to eat to be about half an hour. Feeding them too much is not good for them."

The kids got to see the horses eating their breakfast, since the feed team had left hay "flakes" in the corrals before they had arrived. The tour progressed to the barn where they saw Hope, a six month old filly. The students were very excited to see her. Most had never been around horses at all. Each waited their turn to pet her, and Hope was an eager recipient of the attention. One child exclaimed, "ooh, her nose is sooo soft!"

Hope
Photo Courtesy of WNCR

As the kids moved on to see other horses in their paddocks, Billy was returning from his workout at the circle pen. He was led past the students, who remarked about how beautiful he was.

All the children continued on their tour except for Chad. He watched Billy enter his corral with a ranch hand. Chad approached the fence and stood quietly. Next, another ranch hand also entered the corral with a box of tools. While one ranch hand held the horse with his halter, the other ranch hand with the Feet First Team lifted each of Billy's hooves to check for rocks and clean out the mud.

Billy
Photo Courtesy of WNCR

Chad said. "Why are you looking at his feet?"

The ranch hand replied. "Well, horses can go lame if their hooves have rocks embedded in them. Also, we are checking to be sure their hooves are not cracking or diseased. It is like you taking care of your finger nails or toe nails."

Chad said. "Can I come in and look at them too?"

The ranch hand responded. "I wish you could. But you and your mom need to sign up for orientation and training. Once that is done, you can become a volunteer and enter the corral too."

Chad did not realize that his mom had left the tour as well and was standing nearby observing. She asked. "Is that something you want to do?"

"You bet." He said. "When can we start?"

His mom was so pleased that Chad was showing such interest in horses. His bedroom did have a number of horse books but she thought it was only a passing phase. Now that he showed an interest, especially in this brown mustang, she hoped it might spread to other areas of his life. A spark of light had been re-lit.

Billy approached Chad at the fence and swished his tail. When the ranch hands weren't looking, Chad stuck his hand in the corral and stroked Billy's face. It felt so warm and soft. A small bond of trust was building between the boy and the horse. He was not afraid. The thousand pound horse dwarfed the boy's size, but Chad felt taller than he had in a long time.

Billy nickered a soft sound, which made Chad ask himself. *Was he trying to tell me something?* The horse's jet black eyes looked so soft and kind to Chad. He continued to stroke Billy's face and neck and said. "Well, Billy. Maybe we can become friends. My dad always told me to be kind to others. But it has been difficult since he died. I've been so angry."

CHAPTER 11 – FULFILLMENT

Six months later Billy had become a well-trained horse. He was ready to be adopted and the word got out. Jane and Richard, two volunteers, learned of this and made a bid to adopt him, which the ranch accepted. Jane and Richard considered him to be a valuable animal who didn't have to leave the Ranch, because he had an important job as an ambassador for the ranch.

Billy had fulfilled the goal of the ranch, i.e. rescue these beautiful animals and get them ready for others to enjoy. Billy did not know he was adopted but he loved to be around Jane and Richard. Now retired, they had more time to spend with Billy who they loved.

The trainer used Billy in her classes to help volunteers learn to train other horses. His gentleness made him a favorite of the students who wanted to learn about ground training, the important first step before a horse can be ridden.

Billy continued to be with Chad and his mother as well. They were regular volunteers at the ranch now. Chad, like all volunteers, became very good at mucking the corrals. He and his mom also helped out with feeding. He learned that the young horses and the senior horses ate more often and with special diets, while the other horses ate hay or alfalfa.

Chad took riding lessons and eventually joined Jane on rides near the ranch. They became close friends. She was a good listener, who heard Chad talk often about how proud he was of his father.

Chad was excelling in school once again, and talked about his friends. He often brought them to the Ranch to show off the horses, especially Billy.

Illustration Courtesy of Judy Haag

Chapter 12 – Success

Photo Courtesy of WNCR

Today, Billy continues to live at the ranch. He enjoys the care and attention of the self-less ranch hands who devote themselves to the rescued and abandoned horses who find safety there. Billy's presence is an example of the work done at the ranch as he proudly shows visitors what a beautiful and magnificent horse he is.

BIBLIOGRAPHY

Budiansky, Stephen. *The Nature of Horses: Exploring Equine Evolution, intelligence, and Behavior.*
        New York: The Free Press, 1997.

Help the Pregnant Mares. Accessed May 26, 2014. Available from
        http://www.fourcornersequinerescue.org/slaughtermaresr escue.html

Rounding Up Wild Horses. Accessed November 11, 2013. Available from
        http://www.coboyshowcase.com/roundups.htm

Stop Horse Slaughter. Our Country's Dark Secret. Accessed May 28, 2014. Available from
        http://www.humanesociety.org/issues/horse_slaughter/fac ts/horse_slaughter.html99

State of New Mexico. Animal Cruelty Statute. Accessed May 26, 2014. Available from
        http://nationalaglawcenter.org/wp-content/uploads/assets/animalcruelty/newmexico.pdf

Understanding Horse Behavior. Accessed May 26, 2014. Available from
        http://www.extension.org/sites/default/files/w/2/2b/unde rstanding_horse_behavior.pdf

Walkin N Circles. "Ranch Handbook, " Accessed May 26, 2014. Available from http://www.wncr.org

www.ingramcontent.com/pod-product-compliance
Lightning Source LLC
Chambersburg PA
CBHW042005080426
42733CB00003B/16